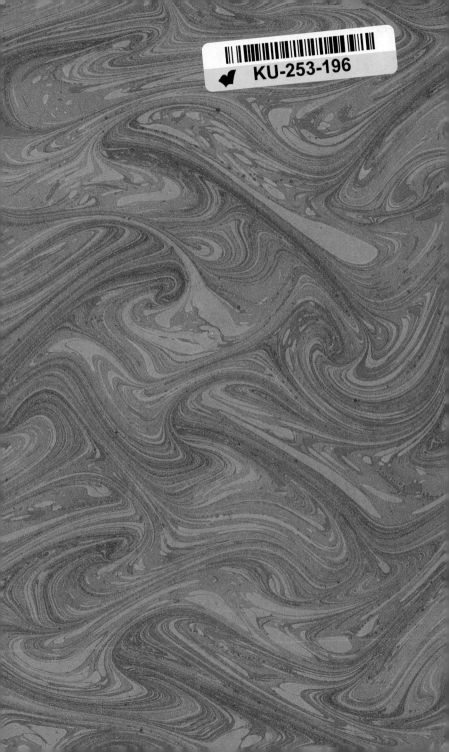

A VICTORIAN POSY

PENHALIGON'S
SCENTED TREASURY
OF VERSE AND
PROSE

Andrea
Preedy
class
A

A Victorian Posy

EDITED BY SHEILA PICKLES

LONDON MCMLXXXVII

For F. Z.

CONTENTS

~INTRODUCTION~

Dear Reader,

My love of scent, of flowers and of poetry has meant that the selection of these floral passages has been a pleasure. I have tried to include some old favourites so there will be something familiar within these leaves for everyone. I have also been careful to include those whose attitudes embodied the Victorian spirit, such as Browning and Hardy, whilst excluding those with more contemporary attitudes, like Vita Sackville-West, even though she was born a Victorian.

I was surprised to find how many Victorian writers personified flowers as children or faeries, and I came to realise that flowers, like scent, are most evocative. They recall in my case the happiest of childhoods; long sunny days playing Hide and Seek in the herbaceous borders or

SPRING

"And in green underwood and cover
Blossom by blossom the spring begins"

CHORUS FROM 'ATALANTA'

For winter's rains and ruins are over,
    And all the season of snows and sins;
The days dividing lover and lover,
    The light that loses, the night that wins;
And time remembered is grief forgotten,
And frosts are slain, and flowers begotten,
And in green underwood and cover
    Blossom by blossom the spring begins.

ALGERNON CHARLES SWINBURNE, 1837-1909

THE SNOWDROP

Yᴏᴜ ask why Spring's fair first-born flower is white:
  Peering from out the warm earth long ago,
It saw above its head great drifts of snow,
And blanched with fright.

Cʟɪɴᴛᴏɴ Sᴄᴏʟʟᴀʀᴅ, 19th ᴄᴇɴᴛᴜʀʏ

ANOTHER SPRING

IF I might see another Spring,
　I'd not plant summer flowers and wait:
I'd have my crocuses at once,
My leafless pink mezereons,
　　My chill-veined snowdrops, choicer yet
　　My white or azure violet,
Leaf-nested primrose; anything
　　To blow at once, not late.

If I might see another Spring,
　I'd listen to the daylight birds
That build their nests and pair and sing,
Nor wait for mateless nightingale;
　　I'd listen to the lusty herds,
　　The ewes with lambs as white as snow,
I'd find out music in the hail
　　And all the winds that blow.

If I might see another Spring—
　Oh stinging comment on my past
That all my past results in "if"—
　If I might see another Spring
I'd laugh to-day, to-day is brief;
I would not wait for anything:
　　I'd use to-day that cannot last,
　　Be glad to-day and sing.

CHRISTINA ROSSETTI, 1830-1894

APPLE-BLOSSOMS

O F all the months that fill the year,
    Give April's month to me,
For earth and sky are then so filled
    With sweet variety.

The apple-blossoms' shower of pearl,
    Though blent with rosier hue,—
As beautiful as woman's blush,
    As evanescent too.

On every bough there is a bud,
    In every bud a flower;
But scarcely bud or flower will last
    Beyond the present hour.

Now comes a shower-cloud o'er the sky,
    Then all again sunshine;
Then clouds again, but brightened with
    The rainbow's coloured line.

Ay, this, this is the month for me:
    I could not love a scene
Where the blue sky was always blue,
    The green earth always green.

LETITIA E. LANDON, 1802-1838

THE FIRST PRIMROSE

HERE we are making the best of our way between the old elms that arch so solemnly overhead, dark and sheltered even now. They say that a spirit haunts this deep pool—a white lady without a head. I cannot say that I have seen her, often as I have paced this lane at deep midnight, to hear the nightingales, and look at the glow-worms; but there, better and rarer than a thousand ghosts, dearer even than nightingales or glow-worms, there is a primrose, the first of the year; a tuft of primroses, springing in yonder sheltered nook, from the mossy roots of an old willow, and living again in the clear bright pool. Oh, how beautiful they are—three fully blown, and two bursting buds! How glad I am I came this way! They are not to be reached. Even Jack Rapley's love of the difficult and the unattainable would fail him here: May herself could not stand on that steep bank. So much the better. Who would wish to disturb them? There they live in their innocent and fragrant beauty, sheltered from the storms, and rejoicing in the sunshine, and looking as if they could feel their happiness. Who would disturb them? Oh, how glad I am I came this way home!

OUR VILLAGE, MARY RUSSELL MITFORD, 1787-1855

VIOLETS

Now a few yards farther, and I reach the bank. Ah! I smell them already—their exquisite perfume steams and lingers in this moist, heavy air. Through this little gate, and along the green south bank of this green wheat-field, and they burst upon me, the lovely violets, in tenfold loveliness. The ground is covered with them, white and purple, enamelling the short dewy grass, looking but the more vividly coloured under the dull, leaden sky. There they lie by hundreds, by thousands. In former years I have been used to watch them from the tiny green bud, till one or two stole into bloom. They never came on me before in such a sudden and luxuriant glory of simple beauty,—and I do really owe one pure and genuine pleasure to feverish London! How beautifully they are placed too, on this sloping bank, with the palm branches waving over them, full of early bees, and mixing their honeyed scent with the more delicate violet odour! How transparent and smooth and lusty are the branches, full of sap and life! And there, just by the old mossy root, is a superb tuft of primroses, with a yellow butterfly hovering over them, like a flower floating on the air. What happiness to sit on this tufty knoll, and fill my basket with the blossoms! What a renewal of heart and mind!

OUR VILLAGE, MARY RUSSELL MITFORD, 1787-1855

BUTTERCUPS AND DAISIES

BUTTERCUPS and daisies,
　Oh, the pretty flowers;
Coming ere the spring-time,
　To tell of sunny hours,
While the trees are leafless,
　While the fields are bare,
Buttercups and daisies
　Spring up here and there.

Ere the snowdrop peepeth,
　Ere the crocus bold,
Ere the early primrose
　Opes its paly gold—
Somewhere on the sunny bank
　Buttercups are bright;
Somewhere 'mong the frozen grass
　Peeps the daisy white.

MARY HOWITT, 19th CENTURY

THE LILY OF THE VALE
Written at nine years of age

SEE, bending to the gentle gale,
  The modest lily of the vale;
Hid in its leaf of tender green,
Mark its soft and simple mien.
Thus sometimes Merit blooms retired,
By genius, taste, and fancy fired:
And thus 'tis oft the wanderer's lot,
To rove to Merit's peaceful cot,
As I have found the lily sweet,
That blossoms in this wild retreat.

MRS. HEMANS, 1793-1835

 SONG

The Return of May

Hail! fairy queen, adorned with flowers,
Attended by the smiling hours,
'Tis thine to dress the rosy bowers
   In colours gay;
We love to wander in thy train,
To meet thee on the fertile plain
To bless thy soft propitious reign,
   O lovely May!

'Tis thine to dress the vale anew,
In fairest verdure bright with dew;
And harebells of the mildest blue,
   Smile in thy way;
Then let us welcome pleasant spring,
And still the flowery tribute bring,
And still to thee our carol sing,
   O lovely May!

Now by the genial zephyr fanned,
The blossoms of the rose expand;
And reared by thee with gentle hand,
   Their charms display;
The air is balmy and serene,
And all the sweet luxuriant scene
By thee is clad in tender green,
   O lovely May!

Mrs. Hemans, 1793-1835

BLUEBELLS
WEDNESDAY 17 MAY 1876

OVER the gate of the meadow there leaned a beautiful wild cherry tree, snowy with blossom, that scented the air far and wide. And along the wild broken bank and among the stems of the hawthorn hedge there grew a profusion of bluebells. I never saw bluebells more beautiful. They grew tall and stately, singly or in groups, and sometimes in such a crowd that they filled the hollow places and deep shadows of the overarching hedge with a sweet blue gloom and tender azure mist among the young bright fern. Here or there a sunbeam found its way through a little window or skylight in the thick leafage overhead and singling out one bluebell amongst the crowd tipped the rich and heavily hanging cluster of bells with a brilliant azure gleam and blue glory, crowning the flower a queen among her ladies and handmaidens who stood around in the background and green shade.

KILVERT'S DIARY, FRANCIS KILVERT, 1840-1879

THE COWSLIP-BALL

A^{T LAST} the baskets were filled, and Lizzy declared victor : and down we sat, on the brink of the stream, under a spreading hawthorn, just disclosing its own pearly buds, and surrounded with the rich and enamelled flowers of the wild hyacinth, blue and white, to make our cowslip-ball. Every one knows the process : to nip off the tufts of flowerets just below the top of the stalk, and hang each cluster nicely balanced across a riband, till you have a long string like a garland ; then to press them closely together, and tie them tightly up. We went on very prosperously, *considering* ; as people say of a young lady's drawing, or a Frenchman's English, or a woman's tragedy, or of the poor little dwarf who works without fingers, or the ingenious sailor who writes with his toes, or generally of any performance which is accomplished by means seemingly inadequate to its production. To be sure we met with a few accidents. First, Lizzy spoiled nearly all her cowslips by snapping them off too short ; so there was a fresh gathering ; in the next place May overset my full basket, and sent the blossoms floating, like so many fairy favours, down the brook ; then, when we were going on pretty steadily, just as we had made a superb wreath, and were thinking of tying it together, Lizzy, who held the riband, caught a glimpse of a gorgeous butterfly, all brown and red and purple, and skipping off to pursue the new object, let go her hold ; so all our treasures were abroad again. At last, however, by dint of taking a branch of alder as a substitute for Lizzy, and hanging the basket in a pollard-ash, out of sight of May, the cowslip-ball was finished.

OUR VILLAGE, MARY RUSSELL MITFORD, 1787-1855

THE RHODORA
ON BEING ASKED, WHENCE IS THE FLOWER?

IN MAY, when sea-winds pierced our solitudes,
I found the fresh Rhodora in the woods,
Spreading its leafless blooms in a damp nook,
To please the desert and the sluggish brook.
The purple petals, fallen in the pool,
Made the black water with their beauty gay;
Here might the red-bird come his plumes to cool,
And court the flower that cheapens his array.
Rhodora! if the sages ask thee why
This charm is wasted on the earth and sky,
Tell them, dear, that if eyes were made for seeing,
Then Beauty is its own excuse for being:
Why thou wert there, O rival of the rose!
I never thought to ask, I never knew;
But, in my simple ignorance, suppose
The self-same Power that brought me there brought you.

RALPH WALDO EMERSON, 1803-1882

THE BALL OF
THE SPRING & SUMMER FLOWERS

HE next person to arrive was the Queen of the Annunciation Lilies. She was dressed in green and silver. "Poor thing," said the young Snowdrops, "she looks so ill and thin. Sitting up late doesn't agree with her." But the Hyacinths, who were young dandies, couldn't take their eyes off her. When the Daffodil came tripping into the room it was the summer flowers' turn to laugh, because, they said, she wasn't young at all, and it was ridiculous at her age to pretend to be a spring flower and to behave like that. The Rose pretended not to see her, and the Lily tossed her head high up in the air and didn't even sniff.

The ball began with a quadrille. The Lizard danced with the Queen of the Lilies, and Prince Fleur-de-Lys danced with the Rose. After that everybody began to dance wildly. The Snowdrops were there in a state of great excitement, because it was their first ball, and their cousins the Crocuses teased and pinched them. The Irises looked at them with contempt as if they were too much used to such things to be excited, although they had only once been to a ball before. The Misses Anemone shivered in the draught, and the Tulips in their crimson and orange tunics danced better than all the young flowers; the lovely Pink, whom everybody was in love with, sat in a corner under a mushroom and talked in a whisper to all the Tulips and the Hyacinths one after another, and the Rose looked at her and frowned, and said it wasn't fair on the Rosebuds and that she ought to be turned out; the Jessamine arrived late, so still and listless, and wandered about looking lonely and pensive, till she found the Lizard, and she talked to him during the whole evening.

THE STORY OF FORGET-ME-NOT & LILY OF THE VALLEY
MAURICE BARING, 1874-1945

Pussy-Willows

B<small>Y</small> the road-side, in the field,
   Greeting each new-comer,—
Pussy-willows wave their plumes,
   Heralding the summer.

A<small>NON</small>

SUMMER

" A thousand flowers – each seeming one
That learnt by gazing at the sun."

⟶⊱ IRREPARABLENESS ⊰⟵

I HAVE been in the meadows all the day,
  And gathered there the nosegay that you see,
Singing within myself as bird or bee
When such do field-work on a morn of May.
But now I look upon my flowers, decay
Has met them in my hands, more fatally
Because more warmly clasped,—and sobs are free
To come instead of songs. What you say,
Sweet counsellors, dear friends? that I should go
Back straightway to the fields and gather more?
Another, sooth, may do it, but not I.
My heart is very tired, my strength is low,
My hands are full of blossoms plucked before,
Held dead within them till myself shall die.

ELIZABETH BARRETT BROWNING, 1806-1861

TO A CHILD

ROSAMUND

THE fairies have been busy while you slept ;
   They have been laughing where the sad rains wept,
They have taught beauty to the ignorant flowers,
Set tasks of hope to weary wind-torn bowers
And heard the lessons learned in school-rooms cold
By seedling snapdragon and marigold.
At dawn, while still you slept, I grew aware
How good the fairies are, how many and fair.

The fairy whose delightful gown is red
Across a corner of our garden sped,
And, where her flying raiment fluttered past,
Its roseate reflection still is cast ;
Red poppies by the rhododendron's side,
Paeonies gorgeous in their summer pride,
And red may-bushes by the old red wall
Shower down their crimson petals over all.

Then she whose gown is gold, and gold her hair,
Swept down the golden steep straight sunbeam stair,
She lit the tulip-lamps, she lit the torch
Of hollyhock beside the cottage porch.
She dressed the honeysuckle in fringe of gold,
She gave the king-cups fairy wealth to hold,
She kissed St. John's wort till it opened wide,
She set the yarrow by the river side.

Then came the lady all whose robes are white :
She made the pale bud blossom in delight,
Set silver stars upon the jasmine's hair,
And gave the stream white lily-buds to wear.
She painted lilies white and pearl-white phlox,
White poppies, passion-flowers and grey-leaved stocks.
Her pure kind touch redeemed the most forlorn,
And even the vile petunia smiled, new-born.

EDITH NESBIT, 1858-1924

A BED OF FORGET-ME-NOTS

Is LOVE so prone to change and rot
We are fain to rear Forget-me-not
By measure in a garden-plot?—

I love its growth at large and free
By untrod path and unlopped tree,
Or nodding by the unpruned hedge,
Or on the water's dangerous edge
Where flags and meadowsweet blow rank
With rushes on the quaking bank.

Love is not taught in learning's school,
Love is not parcelled out by rule:
Hath curb or call an answer got?—
So free must be Forget-me-not.
Give me the flame no dampness dulls,
The passion of the instinctive pulse,
Love steadfast as a fixèd star,
Tender as doves with nestlings are,
More large than time, more strong than death:
    This all creation travails of—
She groans not for a passing breath—
    This is Forget-me-not and Love.

CHRISTINA ROSSETTI, 1830-1894

FLOWER IN THE CRANNIED WALL

FLOWER in the crannied wall
I pluck you out of the crannies
I hold you here, root and all, in my hand
Little flower—but if I could understand
What you are, root and all, and all in all
I should know what God and man is.

ALFRED TENNYSON, 1809-1892

THE COTTAGE

N MY fourth year (autumn of 1827) our family changed house again; father, mother, myself, and a sister a year and a half younger. The move was only across the street, but the new abode, known as The Cottage, had a character of its own. It was an irregularly built house of two stories, with the general shape of the letter L, standing among gardens and shrubberies. The front and the south gable were half-covered with clematis, which embowered the parlour windows in summer; and some wall-trained evergreen fringed the one window of the Nursery with dark sharply-cut leaves, in company with a yellow-blossoming *Pyrus japonica.* Opposite the hall door, a good-sized Walnut Tree growing out of a small grassy knoll leaned its wrinkled stem towards the house, and brushed some of the second-story panes with its broad fragrant leaves. To sit at that little upper-door window (it belonged to a lobby) when it was open to a summer twilight, and the great Tree rustled gently and sent one leafy spray so far that it even touched my face, was an enchantment beyond all telling. Killarney, Switzerland, Venice could not, in later life, come near it . . .

My Father was fond of flowers and we had a good show of all the old-fashioned kinds in their seasons. I loved the violet and lily of the valley, and above all the rose—all roses, and we had many sorts, damask, cabbage, "Scotch", moss, and white roses in multitude on a great shady bush that overhung the little street at our garden-foot. The profusion of these warm-scented white roses gave a great feeling of summer wealth and joy, but my constant favourite was the "Monthly Rose", in colour and fragrance the acme of sweetness and delicacy combined, and keeping up, even in winter time, its faithful affectionate companionship.

A DIARY, WILLIAM ALLINGHAM, 1824-1889

A YELLOW PANSY

O THE wall of the old green garden
    A butterfly quivering came;
His wings on the sombre lichens
    Played like a yellow flame.

He looked at the grey geraniums,
    And the sleepy four-o'clocks;
He looked at the low lanes bordered
    With the glossy-growing box.

He longed for the peace and the silence,
    And the shadows that lengthened there,
And his wee wild heart was weary
    Of skimming the endless air.

And now in the old green garden,—
    I know not how it came,—
A single pansy is blooming,
    Bright as a yellow flame.

And whenever a gay gust passes,
    It quivers as if with pain,
For the butterfly-soul that is in it
    Longs for the winds again!

HELEN GRAY CONE, 19th CENTURY

A Pair of Blue Eyes

Mrs Barbara Worm, not wishing to take any mean advantage of persons in a muddle by observing them, removed her bonnet and mantle with eyes fixed upon the flowers in the plot outside the door. "What beautiful tiger-lilies!" said Mrs Worm. "Yes they are very well, but such a trouble to me on account of the children that come here. They will go eating the berries on the stem, and call 'em currants. Taste wi' juvinals is quite fancy, really." "And your snapdragons look as fierce as ever." "Well really," answered Mrs Smith, entering didactically into the subject, "they are more like Christians than flowers. But they make up well enough wi' the rest, and don't require much tending. And the same can be said o' these miller's wheels. 'Tis a flower I like very much, though so simple. John says he never cares about the flowers of 'em, but men have no eye for anything neat. He says his favourite flower is a cauliflower!"

THOMAS HARDY, 1840-1928

THE POPPIES IN THE GARDEN

THE poppies in the garden, they all wear frocks of silk,
Some are purple, some are pink, and others white as milk,
Light, light, for dancing in, for dancing when the breeze
Plays a little two-step for the blossoms and the bees.
Fine, fine, for dancing in, all frilly at the hem,
Oh, when I watch the poppies dance I long to dance like them!

The poppies in the garden have let their silk frocks fall
All about the border paths, but where are they at all?
Here a frill and there a flounce—a rag of silky red,
But not a poppy-girl is left—I think they've gone to bed.
Gone to bed and gone to sleep; and weary they must be,
For each has left her box of dreams upon the stem for me.

FFRIDA WOLFE, 19th CENTURY

THE POPPY FIELD

ONCE on a time, I know not where,
    I know not when. A dream, may be,
Out of a pine wood, unaware,
    I stepped upon a quiet lea.

And on the quiet meadow I
    Saw all around a carpet spread,
Far as the line where land meets sky,
    Of motionless blown poppies red.

And on the blood-red carpet lay,
    Regarded of a thousand flowers,
A lovely, tired summer day
    In first sleep of the sunset hours.

No breath. No sound. A bird in flight
    The air of evening scarce does cleave,
I scarcely see his stretched wings smite,
    A black line in the fragrant eve.

Once on a time, I know not when,
    Long, long ago. A dream, may be,
But I can see it now as then,
    The silent, purple poppy-sea.

GUSTAV FALKE

THE FLOWERS

ALL the names I know from nurse :
Gardener's garters, Shepherd's purse,
Bachelor's buttons, Lady's smock,
And the Lady Hollyhock.

Fairy places, fairy things,
Fairy woods where the wild bee wings,
Tiny trees for tiny dames—
These must all be fairy names!

Tiny woods below whose boughs
Shady fairies weave a house ;
Tiny tree-tops, rose or thyme,
Where the braver fairies climb!

Fair are grown-up people's trees,
But the fairest woods are these ;
Where if I were not so tall,
I should live for good and all.

ROBERT LOUIS STEVENSON, 1850-1894

A Flower in a Letter

My lonely chamber next the sea
 Is full of many flowers set free
  By summer's earliest duty:
Dear friends upon the garden-walk
Might stop amid their fondest talk
  To pull the least in beauty.

A thousand flowers—each seeming one
That learnt by gazing on the sun
  To counterfeit his shining;
Within whose leaves the holy dew
That falls from heaven, has won anew
  A glory, in declining.

Red roses, used to praises long,
Contented with the poet's song,
    The nightingale's being over;
And lilies white, prepared to touch
The whitest thought, nor soil it much,
    Of dreamer turned to lover.

Deep violets, you liken to
The kindest eyes that look on you,
    Without a thought disloyal;
And cactuses a queen might don,
If weary of a golden crown,
    And still appear as royal.

Pansies for ladies all—(I wis
That none who wear such brooches, miss
    A jewel in the mirror);
And tulips, children love to stretch
Their fingers down, to feel in each
    Its beauty's secret nearer.

Love's language may be talked with these;
To work out choicest sentences
    No blossoms can be meeter;
And, such being used in Eastern bowers,
Young maids may wonder if the flowers
    Or meanings be the sweeter.

ELIZABETH BARRETT BROWNING, 1806-1861

WOMEN AND ROSES

I DREAM of a red-rose tree.
And which of its roses three
Is the dearest rose to me?

Round and round, like a dance of snow
In a dazzling drift, as its guardians, go
Floating the women faded for ages,
Sculptured in stone, on the poet's pages.
Then follow women fresh and gay,
Living and loving and loved to-day.
Last, in the rear, flee the multitude of maidens,
Beauties yet unborn. And all, to one cadence,
They circle their rose on my rose tree.

ROBERT BROWNING, 1812-1889

THERE IS NOTHING HELD SO DEAR

THERE is nothing held so dear
   As love, if only it be hard to win.
The roses that in yonder hedge appear
   Outdo our garden-buds which bloom within;
But since the hand may pluck them every day,
Unmarked they bud, bloom, drop, and drift away.

JEAN INGELOW, 1820-1897

THE MAIDEN

Tess went down the hill to Trantridge Cross, and inattentively waited to take her seat in the van returning from Chaseborough to Shaston. She did not know what the other occupants said to her as she entered, though she answered them; and when they had started anew she rode along with an inward and not an outward eye.

One among her fellow-travellers addressed her more pointedly than any had spoken before: "Why, you be quite a posy! And such roses in early June!"

Then she became aware of the spectacle she presented to their surprised vision: roses at her breast; roses in her hat; roses and strawberries in her basket to the brim. She blushed, and said confusedly that the flowers had been given to her. When the passengers were not looking she stealthily removed the more prominent blooms from her hat and placed them in the basket, where she covered them with her handkerchief. Then she fell to reflecting again, and in looking downwards a thorn of the rose remaining in her breast accidentally pricked her chin. Like all the cottagers in Blackmoor Vale, Tess was steeped in fancies and prefigurative superstitions; she thought this an ill omen—the first she had noticed that day.

TESS OF THE D'URBERVILLES
THOMAS HARDY, 1840-1928

THE WATER-LILY

THENCE, O fragrant form of light,
　Hast thou drifted through the night,
Swanlike, to a leafy nest,
On the restless waves, at rest?

Art thou from the snowy zone
Of a mountain-summit blown,
Or the blossoms of a dream,
Fashioned in the foamy stream?

Nay; methinks the maiden moon,
When the daylight came too soon,
Fleeting from her bath to hide,
Left her garment in the tide.

JOHN B. TABB, 19th CENTURY

THE HONEYSUCKLE

I PLUCKED a honeysuckle where
   The hedge on high is quick with thorn,
   And climbing for the prize, was torn,
And fouled my feet in quag-water ;
   And by the thorns and by the wind
   The blossom that I took was thinn'd,
And yet I found it sweet and fair.

Thence to a richer growth I came,
   Where, nursed in mellow intercourse,
   The honeysuckles sprang by scores,
Not harried like my single stem,
   All virgin lamps of scent and dew.
   So from my hand that first I threw,
Yet plucked not any more of them.

DANTE GABRIEL ROSSETTI, 1828-1882

⤬ GARDEN ROMANCES ⤬

"I HAVE forgotten my flowers," said the spinster aunt.

"Water them now," said Mr. Tupman, in accents of persuasion.

"You will take cold in the evening air," urged the spinster aunt, affectionately.

"No, no," said Mr. Tupman, rising; "it will do me good. Let me accompany you."

The lady paused to adjust the sling in which the left arm of the youth was placed, and taking his right arm led him to the garden.

There was a bower at the further end, with honeysuckle, jessamine, and creeping plants—one of those sweet retreats, which humane men erect for the accommodation of spiders.

The spinster aunt took up a large watering-pot which lay in one corner, and was about to leave the arbour. Mr. Tupman detained her, and drew her to a seat beside him.

"Miss Wardle!" said he.

The spinster aunt trembled, till some pebbles which had accidentally found their way into the large watering-pot, shook like an infant's rattle.

"Miss Wardle," said Mr. Tupman, "you are an angel."

"Mr. Tupman!" exclaimed Rachel, blushing as red as the watering-pot itself.

"Nay," said the eloquent Pickwickian—"I know it but too well."

"All women are angels, they say," murmured the lady, playfully.

"Then what can *you* be; or to what, without presumption, can I compare you?" replied Mr. Tupman. "Where was the woman ever seen, who resembled you? Where else could I hope to find so rare a combination of excellence and beauty? Where else could I seek to—— Oh!" Here Mr. Tupman paused, and pressed the hand which clasped the handle of the happy watering-pot.

PICKWICK PAPERS, CHARLES DICKENS, 1812-1870

UNWATCH'D, THE GARDEN BOUGH SHALL SWAY

From *In Memoriam*

UNWATCH'D, the garden bough shall sway,
　The tender blossom flutter down.
　Unloved, that beech will gather brown,
This maple burn itself away;

Unloved, the sun-flower, shining fair,
　Ray round with flames her disk of seed,
　And many a rose-carnation feed
With summer spice the humming air;

Unloved, by many a sandy bar,
　The brook shall babble down the plain,
　At noon or when the lesser wain
Is twisting round the polar star;

Uncared for, gird the windy grove,
　And flood the haunts of hern and crake;
　Or into silver arrows break
The sailing moon in creek and cove;

Till from the garden and the wild
　A fresh association blow,
　And year by year the landscape grow
Familiar to the stranger's child;

As year by year the labourer tills
　His wonted glebe, or lops the glades;
　And year by year our memory fades
From all the circle of the hills.

ALFRED TENNYSON, 1809-1892

MAUD

COME into the garden, Maud,
    For the black bat, night, has flown,
Come into the garden, Maud,
  I am here at the gate alone;
And the woodbine spices are wafted abroad,
    And the musk of the rose is blown.

For a breeze of morning moves,
  And the planet of Love is on high,
Beginning to faint in the light that she loves
  On a bed of a daffodil sky,
To faint in the light of the sun that she loves,
  To faint in his light, and to die.

All night have the roses heard
  The flute, violin, bassoon ;
All night has the casement jessamine stirr'd
  To the dancers dancing in tune ;
Till a silence fell with the waking bird,
  And a hush with the setting moon.

And the soul of the rose went into my blood,
  As the music clashed in the hall ;
And long by the garden lake I stood,
  For I heard your rivulet fall
From the lake to the meadow and on to the wood,
  Our wood, that is dearer than all ;

From the meadow your walks have left so sweet
  That wherever a March-wind sighs
He sets the jewel-print of your feet
  In violets as blue as your eyes,
To the woody hollows in which we meet
  And the valleys of Paradise.

The slender acacia would not shake
  One long milk-bloom on the tree ;
The white lake-blossom fell into the lake
  As the pimpernel dozed on the lea ;
But the rose was awake all night for your sake,
  Knowing your promise to me ;
The lilies and roses were all awake,
  They sigh'd for the dawn and thee.

ALFRED TENNYSON, 1809-1892

❧ THE DANDELION ☙

W‍ITH locks of gold to-day;
      To-morrow, silver grey;
Then blossom-bald. Behold,
O man, thy fortune told!

JOHN B. TABB, 19th CENTURY

TO A DAISY

THERE is a flower, a little flower
    With silver crest and golden eye,
That welcomes every changing hour,
    And weathers every sky.

The prouder beauties of the field
    In gay but quick succession shine;
Race after race their honours yield,
    They flourish and decline.

But this small flower, to Nature dear,
    While moons and stars their courses run,
Enwreathes the circle of the year,
    Companion of the sun.

It smiles upon the lap of May,
    To sultry August spreads its charm,
Lights pale October on his way,
    And twines December's arm.

The purple heath and golden broom
　　On moory mountains catch the gale ;
O 'er lawns the lily sheds perfume,
　　The violet in the vale.

But this bold floweret climbs the hill,
　　Hides in the forest, haunts the glen,
Plays on the margin of the rill,
　　Peeps round the fox 's den.

Within the garden 's cultured round
　　It shares the sweet carnation 's bed,
And blooms on consecrated ground
　　In honour of the dead.

The lambkin crops its crimson gem ;
　　The wild bee murmurs on its breast ;
The blue-fly bends its pensile stem,
　　Light o 'er the sky-lark 's nest.

'Tis Flora 's page—in every place,
　　In every season, fresh and fair ;
It opens with perennial grace,
　　And blossoms everywhere.

On waste and woodland, rock and plain,
　　Its humble buds unheeded rise ;
The rose has but a summer reign,
　　The daisy never dies !

JAMES MONTGOMERY, 1771-1854

⇢✂ THE GARDENER ✂⇠

THE gardener does not love to talk,
   He makes me keep the gravel walk;
And when he puts his tools away,
He locks the door and takes the key.

Away behind the currant row
Where no one else but cook may go,
Far in the plots, I see him dig,
Old and serious, brown and big.

He digs the flowers, green, red, and blue,
Nor wishes to be spoken to.
He digs the flowers and cuts the hay,
And never seems to want to play.

Silly gardener! summer goes,
And winter comes with pinching toes,
When in the garden bare and brown
You must lay your barrow down.

Well now, and while the summer stays,
To profit by these garden days,
O how much wiser you would be
To play at Indian wars with me!

ROBERT LOUIS STEVENSON, 1850-1894

THROUGH THE LOOKING GLASS

"TIGER-LILY!" said Alice, addressing herself to one that was waving gracefully about in the wind, "I *wish* you could talk!"

"We *can* talk," said the Tiger-lily, "when there's anybody worth talking to."

Alice was so astonished that she couldn't speak for a minute: it quite seemed to take her breath away. At length, as the Tiger-lily only went on waving about, she spoke again, in a timid voice— almost in a whisper. "And can *all* the flowers talk?"

"As well as you can," said the Tiger-lily. "And a great deal louder."

"It isn't manners for us to begin, you know," said the Rose, "and I really was wondering when you'd speak! Said I to myself, 'Her face has got *some* sense in it, though it's not a clever one!' Still, you're the right colour, and that goes a long way."

"I don't care about the colour," the Tiger-lily remarked. "If only her petals curled up a little more, she'd be all right."

Alice didn't like being criticized, so she began asking questions. "Aren't you sometimes frightened at being planted out here, with nobody to take care of you?"

"There's the tree in the middle," said the Rose. "What else is it good for?"

"But what could it do, if any danger came?" Alice asked.

"It could bark," said the Rose.

"It says 'Bough-wough!'" cried a Daisy. "That's why its branches are called boughs!"

"Didn't you know *that*?" cried another Daisy. And here they all began shouting together, till the air seemed quite full of little shrill voices.

"Silence, every one of you!" cried the Tiger-lily, waving itself passionately from side to side, and trembling with excitement. "They know I can't get at them!" it panted, bending its quivering head towards Alice, "or they wouldn't dare to do it!"

"Never mind!" Alice said in a soothing tone, and, stooping down to the Daisies, who were just beginning again, she whispered "If you don't hold your tongues, I'll pick you!"

There was silence in a moment, and several of the pink Daisies turned white.

"That's right!" said the Tiger-lily. "The Daisies are worst of all. When one speaks, they all begin together, and it's enough to make one wither to hear the way they go on!"

"How is it you can all talk so nicely?" Alice said, hoping to get it into a better temper by a compliment. "I've been in many gardens before, but none of the flowers could talk."

"Put your hand down, and feel the ground," said the Tiger-lily. "Then you'll know why."

Alice did so. "It's very hard," she said; "but I don't see what that has to do with it."

"In most gardens," the Tiger-lily said, "they make the beds too soft—so that the flowers are always asleep."

This sounded a very good reason, and Alice was quite pleased to know it. "I never thought of that before!" she said.

"It's my opinion that you never think *at all*," the Rose said, in a rather severe tone.

"I never saw anybody that looked stupider," a Violet said, so suddenly that Alice quite jumped; for it hadn't spoken before.

"Hold *your* tongue!" cried the Tiger-lily. "As if *you* ever saw anybody! You keep your head under the leaves, and snore away there, till you know no more what's going on in the world, than if you were a bud!"

LEWIS CARROLL, 1832-1898

Autumn

" And frosts and shortening days portend
The aged year is near his end."

⚜ THE AUTUMN ⚜

G̲o, sɪᴛ upon the lofty hill,
    And turn your eyes around,
Where waving woods and waters wild
    Do hymn an autumn sound.
The summer sun is faint on them—
    The summer flowers depart—
Sit still—as all transformed to stone,
    Except your musing heart.

How there you sate in summer-time,
   May yet be in your mind;
And how you heard the green woods sing
   Beneath the freshening wind.
Though the same wind now blows around,
   You would its blast recall;
For every breath that stirs the trees
   Doth cause a leaf to fall.

Oh! like that wind, is all the mirth
   That flesh and dust impart;
We cannot bear its visitings,
   When change is on the heart.
Gay words and jests may make us smile
   When Sorrow is asleep;
But other things must make us smile
   When Sorrow bids us *weep*!

The dearest hands that clasp our hands,—
   Their presence may be o'er;
The dearest voice that meets our ear,
   That tone may come no more!
Youth fades; and then, the joys of youth,
   Which once refreshed our mind,
Shall come—as, on those sighing woods,
   The chilling autumn wind.

Hear not the wind—view not the woods;
   Look out o'er vale and hill:
In spring, the sky encircled them—
   The sky is round them still.
Come autumn's scathe, come winter's cold.
   Come change—and human fate!
Whatever prospect HEAVEN doth bound
   Can ne'er be desolate.

ELIZABETH BARRETT BROWNING, 1806-1861

LARK RISE TO CANDLEFORD

N THE last morning of her postwoman's round, when she came to the path between trees where she had seen the birds' footprints on the snow, she turned and looked back upon the familiar landmarks. It was a morning of ground mist, yellow sunshine, and high rifts of blue, white-cloud-dappled sky. The leaves were still thick on the trees, but dew-spangled gossamer threads hung on the bushes and the shrill little cries of unrest of the swallows skimming the green open spaces of the park told of autumn and change. . .

Nearer at hand were the trees and bushes and wild-flower patches beside the path she had trodden daily. The pond where the yellow brandyball water-lilies grew, the little birch thicket where the long-tailed tits had congregated, the boathouse where she had sheltered from the thunderstorm and seen the rain plash like leaden bullets into the leaden water, and the hillock beyond from which she had seen the perfect rainbow. She was never to see any of these again, but she was to carry a mental picture of them, to be recalled at will, through the changing scenes of a lifetime.

As she went on her way, gossamer threads, spun from bush to bush, barricaded her pathway, and as she broke through one after another of these fairy barricades she thought, "They're trying to bind and keep me." But the threads which were to bind her to her native county were more enduring than gossamer. They were spun of love and kinship and cherished memories.

FLORA THOMPSON, 1887-1947

FRINGED GENTIAN

G OD made a little gentian ;
     It tried to be a rose
And failed, and all the summer laughed.
   But just before the snows
There came a purple creature
   That ravished all the hill ;
And summer hid her forehead,
   And mockery was still.
The frosts were her condition ;
   The Tyrian would not come
Until the North evoked it,
   "Creator ! shall I bloom ?"

EMILY DICKINSON, 1830-1886

THE SEA-POPPY

APOPPY grows upon the shore,
Bursts her twin cup in summer late:
Her leaves are glaucous-green and hoar,
Her petals yellow, delicate.

Oft to her cousins turns her thought,
In wonder if they care that she
Is fed with spray for dew, and caught
By every gale that sweeps the sea.

She has no lovers like the red,
That dances with the noble corn:
Her blossoms on the waves are shed,
Where she stands shivering and forlorn.

ROBERT BRIDGES, 1844-1930

THE SONG OF
THE CHRYSANTHEMUM

At last I have come to my throne.
No more, despised and unknown,
In gardens forlorn
My blossoms are born;
No more in some corner obscure
Do I drearily, sadly endure
The withering blight
Of neglect and of slight;
Oh, long have I waited and late,
For this fair and slow-coming fate,
Which the years have foretold
As they sighingly rolled.
Oh, long have I waited and lone;
But at last, on my blossomy throne,
The world doth declare
I am fairest of fair,
And queen of the autumn I reign,
With a sway that none may disdain,—
I, once who did stand,
Despised in the land.

NORA PERRY, 19th CENTURY

IN THE WOOD

IN THE wood where shadows are deepest
From the branches overhead,
Where the wild wood-strawberries cluster,
And the softest moss is spread,
I met today with a fairy,
And I followed her where she led.

Some magical words she uttered,
I alone could understand,
For the sky grew bluer and brighter;
While there rose on either hand
The cloudy walls of a palace
That was built in Fairy-land.

And I stood in a strange enchantment;
I had known it all before:
In my heart of hearts was the magic
Of days that will come no more,
The magic of joy departed,
That Time can never restore.

That never, ah, never, never,
Never again can be: —
Shall I tell you what powerful fairy
Built up this palace for me?
It was only a little white violet
I found at the root of a tree.

ADELAIDE A. PROCTER, 1825-1864

OCTOBER

I ALWAYS long at this time of the year to have been to Japan to see one of their Chrysanthemum shows. I am told our individual flowers are far finer, but their method of arranging the shows is so superior to ours, and the effect produced is naturally much more lovely. They arrange them in bands and waves of colour, from the darkest red to the palest pink, fading into white; and up again from pale lemon, yellow, and orange to the darkest brown. I am sure, even in small collections, picked and unpicked Chrysanthemums look far better if the colours are kept together in clumps, and not dotted about till the general effect becomes mud-colour, as English gardeners always arrange them, only considering their height or the size of their unnaturally disbudded blooms. They are, I admit, most beautiful and useful flowers. What should we do without them? But owners of small places, and I think even large ones, should guard against too much time, attention, and room being given to them. For putting into vases, there is no doubt Chrysanthemums look better allowed to grow more naturally and not so disbudded. A huge Chrysanthemum that is nearly the size of a plate, though it may have won a prize at a local flower-show, looks almost vulgar when picked. Bunches of Chrysanthemums with their buds will go on blooming a long time in water, and make in a room a natural and beautiful decoration, instead of painfully reminding one of the correctness of the flower's paper imitations.

POT-POURRI FROM A SURREY GARDEN, MRS. C. W. EARLE, 1836-1925

TABLE DECORATION

FLOWERS FOR DECORATION should be those which are not very strongly scented. To some the perfume of such flowers as gardenias, stephanotis, hyacinths and others is not offensive, but to others the strong scent in a heated room, especially during dinner, is considered very unpleasant. Otherwise, there is no dictating what the flowers should be. It is well to avoid many colours in one decoration, for, even if well grouped, they are seldom as effective as one or two mixed with white and green. It is a fashion to have a single colour for a dinner-table decoration, this being often chosen of the same tint as the hostess's dress or the hangings of the room, though these are sometimes varied to suit the flowers. Again, all white flowers are very often employed, relieved by plenty of foliage.

MRS. BEETON, 1836-1865

WINTER

"The winter comes: the frozen rut
Is bound with silver bars."

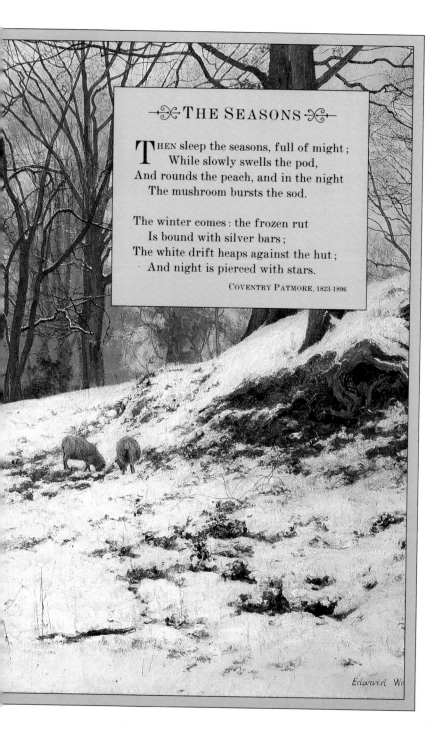

⊸⊱❋ THE SEASONS ❋⊰⊸

THEN sleep the seasons, full of might;
　　While slowly swells the pod,
And rounds the peach, and in the night
　　The mushroom bursts the sod.

The winter comes: the frozen rut
　　Is bound with silver bars;
The white drift heaps against the hut;
　　And night is pierced with stars.

COVENTRY PATMORE. 1823-1896

Edward Wa

JACK FROST IN THE GARDEN

JACK FROST was in the garden;
  I saw him there at dawn;
He was dancing round the bushes
  And prancing on the lawn.
He had a cloak of silver,
  A hat all shimm'ring white,
A wand of glittering star-dust,
  And shoes of sunbeam light.

Jack Frost was in the garden,
  When I went out to play
He nipped my toes and fingers
  And quickly ran away.
I chased him round the wood-shed,
  But, oh! I'm sad to say
That though I chased him everywhere
  He simply wouldn't stay.

Jack Frost was in the garden:
  But now I'd like to know
Where I can find him hiding;
  I've hunted high and low—
I've lost his cloak of silver,
  His hat all shimm'ring white,
His wand of glittering star-dust,
  His shoes of sunbeam light.

JOHN P. SMEETON, 19th CENTURY

＊———— A C O N I T E ————＊

Earth has borne a little son ;
He is a very little one.
He has a head of golden hair
And a grave unwinking stare.
He wears a bib all frilled and green
Round his neck to keep him clean.
Though before another spring
A thousand children Earth may bring
Forth to bid a blossoming—
Lily daughters, cool and slender,
Roses passionate and tender,
Tulip sons as brave as swords,
Hollyhocks like laughing lords—
Yet she 'll never love them quite
As much as she loves Aconite—
Aconite, the first of all,
Who is so very, very small ;
Who is so golden-haired and good,
And wears a bib as babies should.

ANON

WOOD AND GARDEN

THROUGHOUT January, and indeed from the middle
of December, is the time when outdoor flowers
for cutting and house decoration are most scarce;
and yet there are Christmas Roses and yellow
Jasmine and Laurustinus, and in all open weather
Iris stylosa and Czar Violets. A very few flowers
can be made to look well if cleverly arranged with

plenty of good foliage ; and even when a hard and long frost spoils the few blooms that would otherwise be available, leafy branches alone are beautiful in rooms. But, as in all matters that have to do with decoration, everything depends on a right choice of material and the exercise of taste in disposing it. Red-tinted Berberis always looks well alone, if three or four branches are boldly cut from two to three feet long. Branches of the spotted Aucuba do very well by themselves, and are specially beautiful in blue china ; the larger the leaves and the bolder the markings, the better. Where there is an old Exmouth Magnolia that can spare some small branches, nothing makes a nobler room-ornament. The long arching sprays of Alexandrian Laurel do well with green or variegated Box, and will live in a room for several weeks. Among useful winter leaves of smaller growth, those of *Epimedium pinnatum* have a fine red colour and delicate veining, and I find them very useful for grouping with greenhouse flowers of delicate texture. *Gaultheria Shallon* is at its best in winter, and gives valuable branches and twigs for cutting ; and much to be prized are sprays of the Japan Privet, with its tough, highly-polished leaves, so much like those of the orange. There is a variegated Eurya, small branches of which are excellent ; and always useful are the gold and silver Hollies.

GERTRUDE JEKYLL, 1843-1942

WINTER VIOLETS

EATH-WHITE azaleas watched beside my bed,
   And tried to tell me tales of Southern lands;
   But they in hothouse air were born and bred,
And they were gathered by a stranger's hands:
They were not sweet, they never have been free,
And all their pallid beauty had no voice for me.

And all I longed for was one common flower
Fed by soft mists and rainy English air,
A flower that knew the woods, the leafless bower
The wet, green moss, the hedges sharp and bare—
A flower that spoke my language, and could tell
Of all the woods and ways my heart remembers well.

Then came your violets—and at once I heard
The sparrows chatter on the dripping eaves,
The full stream's babbling inarticulate word,
The plash of rain on big wet ivy-leaves;
I saw the woods where thick the dead leaves lie,
And smelt the fresh earths' scent—the scent of memory.

The unleafed trees—the lichens green and grey,
The wide sad-coloured meadows, and the brown
Fields that sleep now, and dream of harvest day
Hiding their seeds like hopes in hearts pent down—
A thousand dreams, a thousand memories
Your violets' voices breathed in unheard melodies—

Unheard by all but me. I heard, I blessed
The little English, English-speaking things
For their sweet selves that laid my wish to rest,
For their sweet help that lent my dreaming wings,
And, most of all, for all the thoughts of you
Which make them smell more sweet than any other violets do.

EDITH NESBIT, 1858-1924

OUTSIDE

KING Winter sat in his Hall one day,
    And he said to himself, said he,
"I must admit I've had some fun,
I've chilled the Earth and cooled the Sun,
    And not a flower or tree
But wishes that my reign were done,
And as long as Time and Tide shall run,
I'll go on making everyone
    As cold as cold can be."

There came a knock at the outer door:
    "Who's there?" King Winter cried;
"Open your Palace Gate," said Spring
"For you can reign no more as King,
    Nor longer here abide;
This message from the Sun I bring,
'The trees are green, the birds do sing;
The hills with joy are echoing':
    So pray, Sir—step outside!"

HUGH CHESTERMAN, 19th CENTURY

—104—

Spring

Stay a Little Longer

"STAY a little longer," said the children to
  the snowdrop,
  "Stay a little longer by the old laburnum tree."
But she said, "I must be going,
Be it hailing, raining, snowing,
I must stir me and be going
For the Master calleth me."

"Stay a little longer," said the children to
  the snowdrop,
"Stay a little longer in your nut-brown nursery."
But she said, "I must be homing
To my sisters in the gloaming,
I must stir me and be homing
For the Master calleth me."

ANON

FLOWER CHORUS

SUCH a commotion under the ground,
    When March called, "Ho there! ho!"
Such spreading of rootlets far and wide,
    Such whisperings to and fro!
"Are you ready?" the Snowdrop asked,
    " 'Tis time to start, you know."
"Almost, my dear!" the Scilla replied,
    "I'll follow as soon as you go."
Then "Ha! ha! ha!" a chorus came
    Of laughter sweet and low,
From millions of flowers under the ground,
    Yes, millions beginning to grow.

"I'll promise my blossoms," the Crocus said,
    "When I hear the blackbird sing."
And straight thereafter Narcissus cried,
    "My silver and gold I'll bring."
"And ere they are dulled," another spoke,
    "The Hyacinth bells shall ring."
But the Violet only murmured, "I'm here,"
    And sweet grew the air of Spring.

O the pretty brave things, thro' the coldest days
    Imprisoned in walls of brown,
They never lost heart tho' the blast shrieked loud,
    And the sleet and the hail came down;
But patiently each wrought her wonderful dress,
    Or fashioned her beautiful crown,
And now they are coming to lighten the world
    Still shadowed by winter's frown.
And well may they cheerily laugh "Ha! ha!"
    In laughter sweet and low,
The millions of flowers under the ground,
    Yes, millions beginning to grow.

RALPH W. EMERSON, 1803-1882

PICTURE ACKNOWLEDGEMENTS

The majority of the illustrations were supplied by Fine Art Photographic Library.

Page 2 J O Banks ; 6 Johann Laurents Jensen ; 9 Joseph Kirkpatrick ; 10 Albert Ernst Muhlig (Gavin Graham) ; 11 John Atkinson Grimshaw ; 13 Christine Marie Loumand ; 14 G Gardner (Chris Beetles Ltd) ; 15 Helen Allingham ; 16 Sidney Shelton (Caelt Gallery) ; 17 Anon : Nister's Annual ; 18 Henry J Johnstone ; 19 Edwin Steele ; 21 Anon ; 23 Myles Birket Foster ; 25 Charles Gregory (Bourne Gallery) ; 27 Arthur John Elsley ; 30 Walter Crane ; 32 George Dunlop Leslie ; 33 Noel Smith ; 35 Henry Wallis ; 37 John Simmons ; 38 Mary Elizabeth Duffield ; 39 Edward Killingworth Johnson ; 40 Arthur Claude Strachan (Galerie George) ; 42 Edmund Julius Detmold ; 45 John H Dell ; 47 Edward Killingworth Johnson ; 48 Emile Vernon ; 49 John Samuel Raven ; 51 Ethel Hughes ; 54 Eva Hollyer ; 55 Edward Killingworth Johnson ; 56-7 E K Johnson ; 58 Vincent Clare ; 59 Henry Ryland ; 60 Frank Percy Wild ; 61 William Jabez Muckley (Cider House Gallery) ; 62 Sophie Anderson ; 63 Anon ; 64 Marcus Shane ; 66 Ernest Walbourn (Cider House Gallery) ; 68 Edward Killingworth Johnson ; 71 William Scott Myles (Anthony Mitchell Paintings, Nottingham) ; 75 Mary Hayllar ; 80 Thomas Creswick ; 88 Anon ; 93 John Ritchie ; 104 Anon : Nister's Annual ; 105 R Drew ; 106 Albert Durer Lucas ; 107 Myles Birket Foster

76 Tenniel from "*Alice Through the Looking Glass*"

79 Edward Wilkins Waite ; 83 Edward Wilkins Waite ; 94-5 Edward Wilkins Waite ; 97 Joseph Farquharson ; 100 Victorian Illustration *Bridgeman Art Library*

20 James T Hart *Bridgeman Art Library/Cider House Gallery*

86 Cesare Saccaggi *Bridgeman Art Library/Galerie George*

72 William Gale *Bridgeman Art Library/Roy Miles Gallery*

65 N Prescott-Davies, 102 M V Morgan ; 109 Mary Ensor *Bridgeman Art Library/Christopher Wood Gallery, London*

89 Richard Doyle *British Museum Prints and Drawings*

29 James Hayllar ; 52 Charles James Lewis *Richard Hagen Ltd, Broadway, Worcs*

91 Marianne North *HMSO/Royal Botanic Gardens, Kew*

70 William Stephen Coleman *Limpsfield Watercolours, Limpsfield, Surrey*

92 from "*Mrs Beeton's Book of Household Management*"

22, 44, 74, 101, 110 *Private Collection, London*

12, 46 *Private Collection, Somerset*

from "*Mrs Loudon's Flower Garden*" pages 7, 78, 84, 85, 98, 99 *Royal Horticultural Society*

PENHALIGON'S

In 1975 Franco Zeffirelli suggested to me that I might like to take over the dying business of Penhaligon's, the perfumery which had been founded a little over a 100 years earlier. By doing so he opened up a whole new world for me. A world of magical scents, mysterious potions, and limitless possibilities. In developing the business, I have tried to live up to the high standard set by its founder William Henry Penhaligon, who left a valuable portfolio of formulae on which to base new perfumes. One of these, Victorian Posy, was created as a result of a request from Dr. Roy Strong, who was planning an exhibition entitled "The Garden" for the Victoria and Albert Museum in 1979 and invited Penhaligon's to celebrate the exhibition by reserving one of our scents for the occasion. I therefore developed Victorian Posy as the most English of scents, for it contains only English country garden flowers, and has the scent of a true Victorian Posy.

Following its success, it seemed natural to complement Victorian Posy by the addition of a book, sweetly scented and reflecting the floral theme.

Sheila Pickles

This edition published in Great Britain in 1987 by
PAVILION BOOKS LIMITED.
196 Shaftesbury Avenue, London WC2H 8JL

10   9

Designed by Bernard Higton
Picture research by Jenny de Gex

British Library Cataloguing in Publication Data

Victorian posy : Penhaligon's scented
treasury of verse and prose.
1. English literature – 19th century
1. Penhaligon's
820 8′008   PR1145

ISBN 1-85145-110-2

Printed and bound in Hong Kong by Imago Publishing Ltd.